THE FREEDOM OF VERSE

Edited by

Zoë Rock

First published in Great Britain in 2000 by
POETRY NOW
Remus House,
Coltsfoot Drive,
Woodston,
Peterborough, PE2 9JX
Telephone (01733) 898101
Fax (01733) 313524

HB ISBN 0 75430 981 9
SB ISBN 0 75430 982 7

FOREWORD

Although we are a nation of poets we are accused of not reading poetry, or buying poetry books. After many years of listening to the incessant gripes of poetry publishers, I can only assume that the books they publish, in general, are books that most people do not want to read.

Poetry should not be obscure, introverted, and as cryptic as a crossword puzzle: it is the poet's duty to reach out and embrace the world.

The world owes the poet nothing and we should not be expected to dig and delve into a rambling discourse searching for some inner meaning.

The reason we write poetry (and almost all of us do) is because we want to communicate: an ideal; an idea; or a specific feeling. Poetry is as essential in communication, as a letter; a radio; a telephone, and the main criterion for selecting the poems in this anthology is very simple: they communicate.

CONTENTS

FREEDOM IS A CAGE

Sitting serene in learned structure,
Cold comforting, an entrenched fort,
Walls secure against threat of rapture,
Chains borne proudly, escape unsought.

Still a shield burdens and falls in time,
The heartfelt longing not to be denied,
Harken to the distant votive chime,
The call proclaims, free will deified.

Learning to be and in being become,
Rise from the swirling primordial,
Walk to the beat of your holy drum.

Yet passing brings a bittersweet sting,
To even bliss we habituate,
Once again needs inchoate stirring,
Leads us quickly to capitulate.

Where once was lush and verdant pasture,
We see a wracked and wretched land,
Beyond redemption beyond fast cure,
A desolation wrought by our hand.

That which we so solemnly cherished,
Showing bold Achilles naked heel,
Its delicate beauty sadly perished.

Pulchritudinous yet still a prison,
Against which just the impotent rage,
Their wayward passion futilely risen,
Like conformity, freedom is a cage.

Peter Walton

Rain

With moods as multifaceted as precious, priceless jewels,
You roam the world revealing wondrous powers.
Within realms equatorial you reign majestically.
In England you fall as sweet April showers.

Along the coast of Florida you team up with the wind,
And cruelly antagonise the sea,
Who rears and writhes in anger, as she rushes at the land,
Creating tragic, human misery.

In tropical savannah summer skies you're thunder rain.
O'er desert, in pure idleness, you laze.
Above the Arctic tundra, freezing land of 'midnight sun',
With snow and wind you're fearsome blizzard-haze.

In cool temperate regions you mischievously appear,
Whether its winter, spring, summer or fall.
Mediterranean blue skies will not allow you in,
So sulkily you make a winter call.

Though man's unique accomplishments, from sphinx to lunar flight,
Cave art to Internet, have brought him fame,
He never will control your moods, gentle or perilous.
Your wanton, wild spirit he cannot tame.

Isobel Stone

JOHN, JOHN

Your breath on my neck,
Fingers running down my leg,
Sweet kisses upon my breast,
Feeling nothing but the best.

The shivers I feel when you're near,
The sound of your voice that I hear,
Your body that I take,
Makes it all, feel like fate.

Falling asleep in your arms,
Makes me feel I'll come to no harm.
I love you with all my heart,
And know that we'll never part.

Whatever the future will bring,
I know we'll get through anything.
Good or bad, I don't care,
With you by my side,
I stand tall with pride.

Stephanie Sharp

CANNOT BE BEATEN
(Inspired by Nelson Mandela)

What cannot be beaten
Your spirits
For if you are strong
Your spirit will fight for you
When life's test forever knocks
Your spirits will embrace you
If sickness call
Your spirit will help you cope
Lean on me
Your spirits will whisper
If you are sinking low
A beam will light up in your heart
And you'll just have to glow
If that smile is fading
A voice will speak to you
Cheer up dear friend
The sun will shine for you
If laughter has walked out the door
Your spirit will find some fun for you
And soon you will be pealing
With sounds of joy

Carolie Pemberton

PEACE A MUST

Show men the way and the path into light
Don't let them stray where their day is like night
Let them go forward without war and its horrors
Give them the strength to keep peace on the morrow.

To war with each other what is it they gain
For surely this killing causes families much pain
To kill and to maim is a blot on our race
Let us live as good neighbours with no such disgrace.

There is never a winner when there comes a truce
For everyone has suffered with this senseless abuse
We must see that the leaders of all the worlds nations
Have a system of peace that is safe for creation.

Lachlan Taylor

BORROWED TIME

Am I the architect of my own heart, a foundation of lives
basis only to be torn
Struggling to build in what I wanted to create, or have I been dying
since the day I was born?
Words seem so strangled, as youth blinds my belief in
becoming a dreamer
Whilst the reality opened up to the truth, and ends my dream
in becoming a believer
Will this become the death of me as I begin to feel
the soil falling over my head,
As closed eyes capture the final sight, will I carry this
catastrophic life to an empty bed.
As I lay alone in my final sleep this emptiness will remain
beyond the end of time
Only sharing my body to the earth that surrounds me as
memories from my soul will always be mine.

As I turned away from it all, the years are felt deep within
The distance of childhood is forever close, and the feeling of
insecurity is lost within.
I'll lose my mind in an unavailing dream, and if it's true I'll never leave
And if I could see colours in a different light, I'll surrender to the
honour and still believe.
As the heart is stripped to reveal a darkness, I realise I'm not half
the man I used to be,
Parted emotions will never return, and I can't replace the tears
from the love that I'll never see.

As night shades over the remaining light, and darkens the soul
of every lonely heart
And the only form of comfort is found in the eyes that have been
crying from the very start.
I'm just like everyone else, I need the feeling to be loved and to
Feel the desire of every need,

I may control my emotions from the tormented past, but if I cut
I still begin to bleed.
A once felt warmth that surrounds the surface, is only touched in the
mid most of my dream
And a sensation that makes me believe I can still feel the pleasures
that it used to seem
I wish I could take away this awkwardness I feel and take me to
a place where no one dies
Where the sounds of laughter form a million smiles and dance before
my open eyes.

A sanctuary built up from a recurring dream, a colony that offers
the release of incessant sorrow
An unveiling mask that's hiding my sadness from the whims of
happiness it echoes in hollow
A sensation that cries from the corners of my mind and rides on
the waves of self deceit
If the future holds the mistakes of yesterday does this mean tomorrow
will never be complete?
As family eyes are turned to blindness, and committed to overlook the
life that they once knew
Will this situation be replaced in time or will my emotions from
the past stand tall.

As memories from a child seem faint and only truly recalling the
isolation of being alone
It's all I can remember from the tears I cried as once the pain is felt
from the emotion I've thrown
As all those around me fall upon high times I call upon the words
I couldn't rhyme
Chasing dreams around a circle of confusement as I begin to feel I'm
living on borrowed time.

My eyes are lying in what I see, as age sets in and the face reveals lines of doubt
Trying to overcome the emotions that ebb and fall as holes appear in the dreams I dreamt about.

Holes in my dream.

Nayland Smith

THE CAROUSEL HORSES

She rides on the carousel horses
Around and around she goes
Dressed all in white with her ribbons and bows
With her lover at her side
She could be one more happy bride
With those stars out tonight
Where she's going to
Only heaven knows.
Standing by the carousel ride
Looking on as those horses go by.
Are those who missed their chances
To fall in love like lovers do
All those who passed her by.
She rides on the carousel horses
Around and around she goes
Dressed all in summer blue.
She rides them alone now
As the sunlight catches her hair
Where she is going to for now
She just doesn't care.
Looking on as those horses go by
Is one lonely child who fell
In love with the stars in the sky.
She knows love is what
Makes the world go by
Love is sometimes lost
Love is sometimes to be found
There on the carousel horses
As they go around and around.

K Lake

MAYTIME

The sun is a friend
on my back,
trees are green castles,
flowers lamps growing
in the grass.
While the world
sings of lilacs
my heart lays down
its winter stones.

Marion Schoeberlein

THERE WAS A TIME

There was a time, not long ago,
When the pace was gentle, very slow,
We had time to stop and chat awhile,
Or walk with friends that extra mile.

There was a time for a quiet stroll,
The only sounds a church bell's toll,
The lowing of cattle, the buzz of a bee,
The song of a bird, wind in a tree.

Now alas the days pass by,
With just a nod, a wave and hi!
And sometimes just a smile,
No time now to walk that extra mile.

Eva A Perrin

STRIPPING

Autumn trees
taking off multi-coloured coats
voluntarily in the weak sun
some as if forced off
by the intrusive early rape of winter,
holding the last remnants close
crying comes late
screaming dissemination of all cover
allowing blanket procreation
earth to new earth
vibrant as in renewal
dusting conception
dying violently to fulfil
bare trees standing in awe.

Robert Shooter

LOST MEADOWS

Whatever has happened?
It puzzles me so.
Now summer is here,
No longer daisy chains
We can make.
So where are 'our' meadows
And fields of long ago
When bluebells and buttercups
We could pick
Sit by a stream - picnic 'to hand'
Listen to the birds
So who has, taken our 'country land'?
Like will-o'-the-wisps,
Property developers
Take over the meadows,
And before our eyes,
Before we realise,
Houses 'shoot up' as if overnight
The daisy chain is broken.
All flowers are gone.
The last word is spoken
For the developers' dream.

Margaret Parnell

RAPUNZEL

This is the Princess Rapunzel so fair,
With long, silky, corn-coloured hair,
Who is locked in a tower that reaches so high,
It almost touches the blue of the sky.

This is the witch, ugly and old,
Who has captured the Princess so we are told,
The Princess Rapunzel who is so fair,
With long, silky, corn-coloured hair,
Who is locked in a tower that reaches so high,
It almost touches the blue of the sky.

This is the Prince so much in love,
Who will rescue the Princess from above,
Who hates the witch, ugly and old,
Who has captured the Princess so we are told,
The Princess Rapunzel who is so fair,
With long, silky, corn-coloured hair,
Who is locked in a tower that reaches so high,
It almost touches the blue of the sky.

This is the window from which hangs the hair,
So the Prince may climb it like a stair,
Yes, the Prince who is so much in love,
Who will rescue the Princess from above,
Who hates the witch, ugly and old,
Who has captured the Princess so we are told,
The Princess Rapunzel who is so fair,
With long, silky, corn-coloured hair,
Who is locked in a tower that reaches so high,
It almost touches the blue of the sky.

These are the scissors which cut the golden locks,
So that the witch could laugh and mock,
At the window from which hangs the hair,
So the Prince may climb it like a stair,
Yes the Prince who is so much in love,

Who will rescue the Princess from above,
Who hates the witch ugly and old,
Who has captured the Princess so we are told,
The Princess Rapunzel who is so fair,
With long, silky, corn-coloured hair,
Who is locked in a tower that reaches so high,
It almost touches the blue of the sky.

Debbie Spink

HILLS

Hills stand above
All the land round about,
We climb them, we cut them
We gouge their sides out.

On top we see distance,
The edge of the earth.
Her length and her breadth
And her quilt-covered girth.

On mist-heavy mornings
They carve through the cloud,
Bones that have broken
Fine threads of a shroud.

Some like to claim them
For country or king,
Others to praise them
And of their might sing.

They force us to raise
Up our eyes to the sky,
The ode of the humbled
Invite us to cry.

And when they're worn flat
By the wind and the rain,
We seek out yet others
To climb up again.

Dave Mountjoy

WAR DANCE

Hear a fire crackle
See the moon begin to rise
And warriors are dancing
Honour gleaming in their eyes

Camouflaged in starlight
Weapons hungry for the kill
Anticipating fresh blood
That's so very soon to spill

War cries on the lips of men
Who wear the battle's mask
Allegiance pledged to Erin
And whatever she may ask

Brave men with the strength of giants
Beating in their hearts
And when the bodhran stops
That is the time the fighting starts.

Kim Montia

AUTUMN

Putting aside
Last rays of summer sun,
Shrouded in mist
With hint of cold to come,
Stands Autumn,
The Evening of the year.

Gathering the
End of summer's fruitfulness,
The peak of swollen ripeness,
Not yet slipping to decay,
Is Autumn
The fulfilment of the year.

Damping down sap
As gold leaves crunch and crinkle,
Signalling time to sleep
Or fly away,
Is Autumn,
Preparing for
The ending of the year.

Anne Cryer

MOTHER SPIDER

Her moon-like, shadowy thread,
Weaves gracefully through the grass blades,
Callously forgetting,
That one snapped link,
Will sabotage the rest of her artwork.
The cosmos, sustained and intertwined
As those blades of grass.
Fragile, dependent on each part of the universe,
As a united body.
United, yet so far distanced.
How will we know,
The extent of the damage
We have reeked upon the cosmos?
Like a small, naive child,
Running through the garden,
Dashing the web against his Adidas trainers . . .
Stranger still,
How this planet's web is held together,
By something as simple and insignificant,
As a cloud.

Kim Huggens

TESTING TIMES

Long ago when I went to school
'Progress Papers' were the rule.
Children sat at lonely desks
Aiming for the perfect test.
Jumping through hoops for some reward.
A new bike and a future if you worked hard.
Deciding destinies at eleven,
Now the failing starts at seven.
What is the criterion for success?
A few may meet it, but what of the rest?
At best they're in line with the average score,
At worst they'll have to do a whole lot more
Just to get a Level Four.

Don't you feel concerned about the SATS
Changing lovely children into brats?
'I am better, cleverer than you
You're the thickest kid in school.'
And later when they've left school behind,
Don't be surprised when they're unkind
Failing time and time again
Not so good for self-esteem.
Inadequate, sad and insecure,
Do I have to spell out more?
What levels are gained for demonstrating sharing
For being kind and being caring
For being happy and bringing joy to others
For looking out for sisters and brothers?
If we only measure their success in tests,
Then that is what they will learn to do best.

L A Grewer

CROW'S END

A crow dangled darkly
below its stark nest.
Alone and deserted,
its claw trapped forever
fixed to the woven twigs,
raucously screaming
till merciful rest.

A crow dangled stiffly
in the still cold day.
A reminder, a warning
its own brief life ending,
bereft of all beauty
with rigid wings helpless
in staring decay.

A crow dangles grimly
from fingers of death.
Trapped by its fickle home,
blended and twisted,
at one with its shelter,
it cursed its surroundings
with last fetid breath.

A crow's body dangles
as black flag to the sky.
Shunned by the spiny leaves,
withered by chilling wind,
grotesque and revealed
on a gibbet of nature
to all that pass by.

Ian Fisher

RACIAL HATRED

The savage hate pervades tortured soul
with threat it squints to reveal lantern jaw,
displays steely knuckles that lose control -
that have maimed others - many times before.

The awesome gaze, much safer to deny
when body collides against sweating skin,
this racial violence, one ponders why,
it could be fruit from his ignorant kin.

Its snarling voice, it's wiser not to hear
the glinting knife, so surely you will see,
as unspoken words compound the fear
of some brutish maim - that is yet to be.

If one should resist, you may count the cost
as your life of living - may soon be lost.

Alex Branthwaite

Nature's Busy Ways - At Work!

This day is bright - sun full out - nature's ways are busy -
at their work - busy bees visit waiting flower beds -
birds of heaven looking for needed food -
I too am awake to see the wonders of nature's ways -
eyes, eager to see the wonders - the details of her ways -
true - man's hands play a part - cut the grass -
tidy up the flower beds and he can plant - and he can sow -
the hand of nature must do the rest - she takes no days off
to rest awhile - she is working while we sleep
even in the autumn days she has her work cut out -
true - a time is given for her to rest her growing ways -
to restore her strength for another coming year when -
once again - she will show our world she is busy at her work.
Spring will see new signs of life. Summer - a time to show
the glory of her growing ways. Autumn to rest awhile
before days of Winter - that time for needed rest again -
how can I say this is just another day? -
It is indeed a part of a whole year -
that play a part in nature's busy ways - at work.

R P Scannell

THE JUNK MAIL

Waking in the morning, what was that I heard?
It was the letter box clinking
Wondered what was there
Going to retrieve the post
Looking through the mail
Nothing there I wanted

Offering of credit card, books and catalogues
Some saying you're a winner
Not that I can see
If I was a winner
Why did they not send it direct to me?
What a waste of time to send us all this trash
Just to keep the dustbin full
Oh, such a waste!

Irene Pierce

UNTITLED

Do not seek redemption,
because she hunts all those
who have earned her swiftness.
Invited or not, as the shining sword
of cosmic justice, she strikes.
To the very heart of the dark side of wrong-doing.
Truth is her reason,
your action her cause.
Weakness is your downfall,
and with this redemption is upon you.

Simon King

IMAGININGS

Hush, is that I noise I heard
No maybe it is just a bird
I must be imagining things
Did that toy telephone ring?

Come on, pull yourself together
This is not being very clever
I am looking after a very old house
Me and I am even afraid of a little mouse

There is a movement by the toys
That is where I heard that noise
Why did I agree to house sitting
I can hear my heart beating.

This house is very old and bleak
Did I hear the floorboard creak?
It is gone really dark
Did I hear the dog bark?

Is that a shadow I see
I am being silly, it is only me
I know I am not going to last the night
I am really going to die of fright

There is definitely a noise
And there are shadows over by the toys
I think there are spirits over there
I am going to run if I dare

I am feeling all hot and I am rooted to the spot
I open my eyes and take a deep sigh
It is my friends, I laugh and cry
It is only a joke and I am not going to die.

D A Fieldhouse

LEFT OF TRUTH (CARVED ISOLATION)

Carved isolation contaminates the soul,
As all we heard in safety destroys the vacant whole,
Reserved truths now emerge all as one,
Victory reigns emptily now honesty is gone.
Ever and forever, such things we cannot see,
Dying and decayed inside for all we cannot be,
Implied reasoning obliterates the old,
Such a careless living now the sacrosanct is sold.
Only ever after was all but promised lies,
Lack and evolution destroyed all alibis,
An always eternal pleasure to endure,
The last remaining hope holds master of the door.
If trust could be regained and falsity replaced,
One of these broken models could vanish without trace,
Now we see the future to frighten all with view,
If an if only seem all that is (left) of truth.

Helen Marshall

MAMA WENT HOME TODAY

Mama went Home today . . .
She died in Peace.
Finally, sweet release.
I can see her now,
with her smiling brow.

With Jesus holding her,
in His strong arm.
Now she's safe and free
from all alarm.

Carol Olson

EXIT LEFT

Exit left
For the final curtain call
Remember past times
When laughter drove away the pain
I am laughing now, not at you
But with you
Walk away, look at the sky
Even if it's pouring
Let raindrops fall on your face
A reminder of all the tears
Which have been shed in this place
But
Tomorrow the sun will shine
Only death
Destroys the appetite for life
Enjoy it
There is no disrespect in being hungry
The curtain's down
The audience have gone away
Until called
Their part to play . . .

Jim Parkinson

SELBY
(My home town)

Grandad came from Ireland to find work in the town,
which once was full of industry for everyone around.

Nestling on the River Ouse, a busy port of call for vessels
carrying many goods, some large ones and some small.

Cochrane's were the shipbuilders known wide and far,
for their high standard workmanship and special unique way
of launching all ships sideways which made the river sway.

The river is much quieter now the shipyard long gone,
but some things are still the same and some are going just as strong.

The market on a Monday brings people from around,
looking for a bargain, trying to save a pound
on anything from bric-a-brac, stylish things to wear,
even roasted chestnuts on a cold and frosty day.

The ancient Abbey stands there with all its history,
stained-glass windows repaired not long ago,
when fire engulfed the building and set it all aglow.

We have to maintain it to make sure it's always there,
for future generations celebrating happy times and sad
to know we've taken care of it can only make them glad.

The park is really beautiful when everything's in bloom
and there is nothing better on a sunny afternoon,
you can sit and watch the bowling, see the kids at play,
find yourself a shady tree to keep the sun at bay.

When autumn leaves have fallen, frosted trees are white,
we'll prepare for Christmas and cover them with lights.

Patricia Trickett

Months Of The Year

What are the months all about?
There's January which is cold and wet.
February with the roses and chocolates set.
March which comes in like the wind and out like a breeze,
but April sees me a'plenty, a'pleased.
May is the month with flowers in bloom
and June can be considered quite a gloom.
July is the season to be happy, for school is out
and summery August is coming about.
September comes and goes like the setting of the sun,
but October sees lots of goblins and ghoulish fun.
Then it is 'remember, remember, the 5th of November'
But then it is Christmas, which falls in December!

Jessica Murch

THE DORSET MARTYRS

Tolpuddle, Dorset, is their shrine,
Loveless, Hammet, Standfield and Brine,
Victims were they of Whiggery,
And Squire Frampton's skulduggery.

Farm labourers and nothing more,
That in the March of thirty-four,
At Dorchester Assizes met,
John Williams and John Bosanquet.

Before these justices of court,
A fair deal was all they sought,
Against a life of degradation,
Low wages, poverty and starvation.

That Union oath, their only crime,
A seven-year sentence, was their time,
Found guilty of a felony,
Transported far across the sea.

A plea for mitigation fails,
Five banished off to New South Wales,
To Strathallan, Glindon and Maitland,
George Loveless to Van Dieman's Land.

In Eighteen thirty-six they won
From the King, a free pardon,
And for the government, also please,
Leave from the Antipodes.

To England they could now return,
Where for them a torch would burn,
On native soil, they were now free,
To claim their birthright, *Liberty!*

John Bradley

DAWN

Dawn, the sun slowly rises,
Over the black, cold night of despair
Grey, turns to day
Orange, red, yellow
Hit my soul, with painful intensity
I gaze out at my thoughts
Watching them chance to blue
A pure, peaceful, mellow blue
And the waves lap gently, on my heart
Washing the pain
With an easy persistence
As the peace takes over, and stills the beating wings
The butterfly of my heart stills
And as I rest, I gaze into the brown pools of your eyes
I swim, and drink, and languish
Pushing away the total anguish, hurt, pain
Confusion and frustration, melting
As the bird soars, free
A new day has begun
And you, in my life have become the sun.

Cate Campbell

THE ONLY WAY

A friend does not have to
thank a friend
Because they're always in
their mind
When you help a friend in need
In their mind they know you're kind.

When you help a friend who has
lost their way
All the money in this world
Would not be enough to pay.

But a 'thank you' in your dear
friend's mind
Will be the only way.

Bert Booley

A TRANQUIL MOMENT

Strolled onto the banks of a stream
Sat watching the long grass swaying.
Ivy trailing and twining along the brook,
Beautiful breeze, so fresh.
The bluebells in and amongst other sprouting leaves.
Dandelions popping up here and there,
Cascade of blushing bright yellow mustard in fields nearby.
Delicate fragrances from the lilac bushes,
And wallflowers filling the air.
Lovely blue skies, the birds singing.
I sigh and think to myself,
The highs and lows of everyday life,
Is what life is all about.
Looking across onto the moors and valleys,
The stretches of scenery,
So tranquil, so peaceful.
Sun shining so brightly,
Just like the flames of a fire.
What a feeling!
As I walk away, I feel the loveliness
Of the blooming colours springing into life,
And count my blessings,
I am so proud of my very own blossoming roses.
Every bit my pride and joy,
My lovely daughters,
All I am living for, they are my world!

Always and forever loving you with all my heart 'darlings'
love Mum.

PS 'So long as I am around, I will never let my roses wither.'

Yasmin Aysha Suraiyya

YELLOW CARD

Sitting in front of the telly
Watching the football one night,
Shaking my head at low tackles
And players who started a fight,
I'd a tray on my knee
With a jigsaw half done.
I'd been struggling to fit in the pieces
But now, I was certain I'd won.
Next thing I fell into a slumber.
How long I was out I don't know.
I awoke with a start at midnight
And I wasn't quite 'all systems go'!
I had just one thought in my head
As I leapt to my feet half asleep,
That was, to put down the puzzle
And under the blankets to creep . . .
I completely forgot that footstool!
Right under my nose it lay.
I flew head over heels on my bottom,
What a stupid, daft piece of foul play!
There was blood everywhere on the carpet
From a gash in front of my shin;
But I didn't drop one bit of jigsaw
I'd managed to keep them all in!
It cost me three weeks with my leg up,
I'd time to do puzzles galore.
And one thing I'm certainly sure of . . .
I know what a yellow card's for!

Evelyn Balmain

THE STRANGER WAS MY DAD

Who were you in all those years
We sat at the same table?
What did you think?
I never knew, though physically capable
You opened to no feelings,
Engaged in no conversation,
Left no clue; came and went
Like a windowless soul well hid from view.

Who were you in all those years,
When I had such need for sharing?
Would reach out, though never got near.
See you withdraw,
Leave, reject, become deaf
With a look of anguished fear drain across your face.
That was the little I saw.

Who were you in all those years
When unsupported I left the coldness of home
Where none expressed real care
Or placed their hurts upon the table?

Your final hour saw retribution,
Sorrow at your loss.
A love-need showing, surpassed the hurts
As all negated goodness, revealed the cost,
Came to the fore in knowing,
That omission was your only sin
Seeking amendment before your going
To the grave. I could hardly bear it.
Too late to crave, too late to knock on life's door.
You departed, and left my heartache sore.

Who were you Dad, the stranger in my life.

Marion Elvera

SILENT MAJORITY

What an event
This millennium does hold
Remembering Dunkirk evacuation
No matter how old.

This Sunday holds
Remembering vet'rans of Dunkirk
Who evacuated soldiers
In their escape work.

Such pride bestowed
On those silent lost lives
Who never again did see their
Children, mothers, wives.

Honour oozes
Today on Dunkirk beaches
So the rescuers travelled
Within the boat's reaches.

The Germans had been slow
Ground down to actual stop
All those sixty years ago
When the Germans did flop.

The veterans jog mem'ry
Oh the shame on us!
How could we forget it all
This wonderful fuss?

The finality of goodbye!

Barbara Sherlow

CALL ME NOW

I'm sitting by the telephone wishing you would call
The time goes by so slowly I feel so sad and small
I don't think that you love me or care for me at all
You're busy with your own lifestyle and thoughts of me let fall

Oh, how I think about you and wish that you were here
You may not know it, but for you my love's sincere
I'm sure you keep so busy and when you drink your beer
This little lonely lady is filled with lots of fear

You told me you are lonely and have no one to love
I wish that you would phone me, your little turtle dove
The cost is only four pence and I'm sent from up above
I'll pay the four pence for you, don't you think that's true love?

I'm fed up waiting for you, I've got to go to bed
I'll lie awake a'while and think of all you've said
I've turned the telly off now and paper books I've read
And now I know just what to do, *I'll just ring you instead!*

Muriel Turner

THE SEA

What myriad eyes have looked in awe upon its glorious sight,
What countless souls have ventured on its furling waves
In vain to think that they could tame its might
Its surging, lifting, billowing to the height
And ebbing into countless unseen caves

A thousand shadows dwell beneath its foam
And shoot and dart and scurry in their shoals
And fronded urchins dance and play their parts
Swaying and bending in their roles

The rafts and oars and tall ships chanced their way
And stretched their heaving sails into the hungry winds
Which roared and raged and snatched the canvasses in tortuous gales
And Neptune watched and laughed as strivings failed
And groaning timbers vanished to the deep
And waited in their long and timeless sleep

The fathoms dark and spectral, shrouded hulls
That long since plied their trades to cloistered bays
Captained by intrepid salts of old
Who journeyed with their spoils of yesterday
And took their creaking crafts across the main
And filled their greedy coffers with its gold

And great men through the years have played their part
In fighting nature's unrelenting storms
And made their voyages with heart
And ridden nights of black, and golden dawns
Each adding names to that most glorious roll
Of honourable ventures for the soul.

But still the sea, its reign supreme, continues to elude man's puny hand
And crashing, heaves and spreads its thunderous way
And breaks the slippery ropes of tenuous strand
And mightily triumphant holds its sway
In awesome majesty, against the soft and timorous land.

Barbara J Settle

THE SILVERING

Late in May;
Windy day;
Floods high from the west,
Hillsides grappling;
Bend the sapling,
Broods fly from the nest!
When one day;
Begone the grey,
In a blinding sun;
Brilliant lighting;
Silver brightening,
Then the cloud is gone!
Across the Vale;
Lights prevail,
Under clearest view;
Silver lining,
Shadows running;
Wonder . . . deepest blue!

Tom Ritchie

MAY CLOSES

May closes, only time has stood still
As though being merely a snapshot
It could be December the ending of the year.
The weather's altered yet chilled are his thoughts.
Flowers swathed in brilliant sunshine
Sway helplessly in May's gusty breeze.
And from the window where he sits,
Looking into the distance, all has spring's
Array of vibrant colour, yet his mental horizon
Is barren. May and December have merged
And winter's bleakness holds court.

Beauty cannot exist when the soul's filled with hate
And seasons merely reflect one's mental state
People are company only when needed,
And life's only lived when the seasons are heeded.
Where love had dominated and given vigorous
                           strength to his being
Another had drained by lying and deceiving
She had left with another when all had become clear
And pure hate like December's ice did suddenly appear.
May will turn to June, and time will merrily dance on,
But a broken heart will only mend when the
                           memories have gone.

Shaun Hillen

HAPPINESS

We sat and we talked
The old man and me
Of life and love
And people who see.

He talked of the woman
He'd loved through the years
'She's gone before me'
He said through his tears.

'But she'll be waiting
for me never fear
We made a promise
To always stay near.

Children can hurt you
Expecting too much.
When all you want
Is a smile and a touch.'

Then he looked at his dog
As it sat at his feet
'They're faithful you know
Real hard to beat

And the spirit you have
Will always survive
But then I've had love'
He said with great pride.

I asked about happiness
And he looked in my eyes
'That's something you don't
Know you have, till it's gone.'

I thought on his words as I
Went on my way
and decided I will be happy today.

Joan May Wills

FOLLOWING FORKED TONGUE

After nights and weeks of
He being tiger and
I being snakes,
We enter into these lifts of limbo.
I've given up my venom and rattle,
Yet in doing so they seem
To have dissolved inside
Instead of outside of me -
Fused me into a mixture of
Acid and spite and
Sick, milky lethargy.
They have corroded the weight in me
And now I've lifted,
Left my belly on the floor
While my limbs, wrists and ankles
Press the ceiling.
I imagine what she would
Say to me, perhaps,
'Now, that's what you get for
Not properly disposing of venom, girl.'
Well, maybe his stripes
Are up here somewhere, and can
Cut this nothingness into
Something like love.

Erin Halliday

ROMEO AND JULIET
(The Moon And The Sun)

Do rainbows form the arch,
Of the sun and moon's love,
In a letter written by the rainfall,
And read by the clouds from above?

Does each colour represent
The thoughts of the two, who
                    choose to give light,
One in the hours of the day
And the other throughout the night.

Who together, share in the power,
Of instilling in life - that growth
                    may give birth,
Under the guidance of 'Mother Nature'
Owner of the largest garden on earth.

The 'orange' - and the 'lemon',
Who have brought warmth and affection,
Too many young hearts as of a need,
Teaching those of like minds -
- In each other - to love - and to believe.

Bakewell Burt

PALACE

You're a tender thing, to which is true
And your life is my joy, and to say 'I love you'

But you're too far away, and my heart cannot resist
In this wonderless world it is you that exists

I've taken a breath, and a stance is mine
So I hold out my hand, for now and all time

And when that time is present, you will give yourself to me
Our lives will be complete, in perfect harmony.

Alex Mcleod

SMALL, FURRY AND LIVING NEARBY

Are mice leaving taste-holes in apples -
And foxes that drink from a fish pond.
Moles undermine lawns, and then abscond.
Above ground lies soil they grappled

With down below, telling the tale
Of the old muddy mountain. Gymnastic
Grey squirrels are enthusiastic
About larger gardens, where they scale

Ridged bark of tall trees planted young
In the inter-war years, or linen lines -
A squirrel's direct route to nuts hung
For blue tits; and coconuts on twine.

Evening trains run, but don't scare rabbits
Back into their warrens. Short-tailed voles
Risk ventures from cutting bank holes.
Though stalking's one of a cat's habits.

Gillian C Fisher

DESOLATION

This is a cold desert
Grey, dust choking -
Unremitting cold sharp winds.
Ever in a stone-grey twilight,
Eternal dead evening
With dark lowering clouds
Glinting, steel-edged
Against a bitter sky.
To be here is to be lost -
There are no landmarks,
No paths in the drifting dust
Between the jagged rocks,
No tracks but my own,
No journey's end
Beyond the stark horizon.

Margaret Blake

TROLLEY MANIA

It had to come, did Trolley rage, to be part of a modern trend
And now even non-motorists can vent their anger - two fingers
to extend.
There could be a section set aside for a motorised practice run
So instead of spending money reluctantly - shopping will be fun
Children no longer dragged around - they'll look forward to the day.
There will of course be certificates of excellence before L plates are
taken away.
No longer will there be frustration with that trolley having a mind
of its own.
The one that's caused chipped ankles and more than just a moan.
What with computers and now our own vehicular shopping facility,
We should all be so very happy - we will have to wait and see.
There will certainly be more excitement as some demand an increase
in speed
And the proficiency of the enthusiast gets out of hand to be always
in the lead.
Was it such a good idea? We have to be prepared to give it all a try.
What could be next? Perhaps trolley sharing with even more chaos
for you and I.

Reg Morris

MADAM DRAGONFLY

Nature is indifferent in ideology
Brownmiller or anthropology
A dilemma for sociologists,
An enigma to biologists.

She has no concern for the future
She creates. She nurtures. She destroys.
And Mankind in awe, can only wonder
About the method she employs.

Yet we deny our own humanity!
With this 'debunk Darwin'! vanity.
And led by the nose to moral stagnation,
With furious feminist incantations.

Olde worn-out dogma and platitudes
Will never change social attitudes.
Brownmiller before everything.
Domination?
'Specialised rape organ'?
Abomination . . .!

Feminists please! Don't take offence,
But your rationale, does not make sense.
By ignoring opinion and stifling debate
Is to leave the future in the hands of
Fate.

And men would end 'In-Vitro' swimming,
In Brownmiller's Amazonian
World of
Women . . .!

Michael John McKay

An Awful Lot Of Hell

I walk the walk
And talk the talk
And sniff the sweet
Cocaine
I used to
A 'used-to-be'
And that's my claim to fame
I'm not a fool
I read the news
'I know' precisely
What I risk
But this sad
Obituary
Is really quite a list
Still I'll walk the walk
And talk the talk
Until the day
I die
A waste of space
And energy
A 'Lucy in the sky'
But I'm not a child
I know the score
And I know you
Mean it well
For a little bit of
Paradise
That's an awful lot of hell.

Rod Trott

THANK YOU III

Thank you for reviving me
With your love and chosen words
Thank you for holding me
As gently as a bird

Thank you for your uplifting smile
Upon a face not so pure
Thank you for your warming touch
From the hand that reassured

Thank you for my days of grace
With culture at my side
Thank you for the warmth of your heart
And my love that never died

Thank you for your openness
To fill the empty pages
Thank you for your sophistication
And everyone of its stages

Thank you for your gracious time
When the days never fell short
Thank you for your Spanish eyes
Which we need not import

Thank you for your honesty
When mine lay spent
I thank you not for my tears
Because my love was content

Warren Brown

Will My Sadness Ever Go Away

Oh my cherished mother how I miss thee
Treasured angel where can you be?
Each night I watch the stars above
Searching for you, for I need your love.
It's knowing that you're not really far away
That helps me through each lonely day.
I can feel your presence when I'm alone
I can smell your belongings about my home.
Your photographs are everywhere
For me to treasure, they help be bear.
Your passing from this world oh Mom
It breaks my heart, where have you gone?
For it's not easy, yet people say
Those tearful nights will pass away.
But how can they ever understand
How much I loved you, it's so hard to stand.
Those empty feelings so deep inside me
That where you are I long to be.
No one had ever prepared me for such a loss
Or made me realise just how much I'd got.
I pick up your photo, my fingers trace
Across that wisdom that was your face.
Deep in those old eyes I see
A pictured image that could be me.
You gave so much yet asked for nothing Mom
And now from me your soul has gone.
All the books in the world could never explain
The loss of a mother, that agonising pain.
Thank God for my poetry for it helps me express
My overwhelming feelings about life and death.

God bless you my sweet mother, it was so
Hard for me to write this.

Ann Hathaway

ELVA

You are an aunt I hold so dear.
The one who helped a girl so young,
Within the heated rays of the wild,
You gave me hope for a future bright.

You walk in beauty, like the stars,
Of cloudless nights and starry skies,
And all that's best of dark and light,
Meet in the twinkle of your eyes.

Now while the summer stays,
You profit by the garden days.
Aunt Elva you will always be
Brave and wise and true at heart.

Carol Gilby

THE BUZZARD'S NEST!

In the hall of my memories when I was a child
With Aly I'd ramble to hills that beguiled
Concealed diamond lochans held sparkling fish
Wild trout we would tickle for our mothers' dish

One day we had made of brown trout a fine catch
Strung through their gills, like brown keys for a latch
We topped a high gully with startled surprise
A mighty brown bird from its nest did arise

We scrambled down wildly and fell by the tree
Up high in its arms its nest we did see
We climbed the tall tree as the sky for a guide
Three specked gems in the nest lay inside

They lay in the nest like three gems on a gown
A rustic twigged cloak to be worn with a crown
We stole the crown jewels from that mighty bird
And climbed back down slowly with never a word

We started home slowly with treasure in store
Our covetous gaze on the eggs did outpour
The buzzard sailed over with mewling cries wild
That seemed like the cry of a lost frightened child

We stopped in our tracks as our conscience did throb
We knew in our hearts, we had no right to rob
Shamed by our theft we returned to the tree
And replaced the gems, that in number were three

We started on homewards and then by and by
A twig fell beside us from out of the sky
Al picked it up then it passed to me
The buzzard sailed over had thanked us you see

Roy A Millar

ORIENTAL FAVOURITE

Soft and caring lovely creature,
Sitting purring on my knee.
Big blue eyes, a startling feature,
Why bestow your favours on me.

Happily sitting, watching,
While I pour you out a dish of cream.
Realising your position,
Tall and regal, you are a queen.

Contented now, you wash your face
And curl up to have a sleep.
Doing everything with grace,
Dignity is yours to keep.

Gently then, I stroke your coat,
Relaxed and happy as I do.
Trusting companion never remote,
My Siamese, no cat is like you.

Katrina M Anderson

MOTHER'S DAY

Your mum is the best friend
you could ever have,
through all the bad times, sad times,
she has been there,
a shoulder to lean on
when I'm in despair.
Mum, I will always be there
to show you that I care,
expressing the love we both share.
Through our lives there have been
good times and bad,
it's just a part of life,
it's quite mad.
I think we are here to be put to the test,
so from now on, I'm going to do my best.
Thanks for your guidance
throughout my life Mum.

Julian Thorpe

ROSES

I will find you, my turn will come,
There are all kinds of roses,
I will count them one by one.

The rose voice,
Out of each rose 'tower'
Will be the scent
of every rose - bower.

And so at last, white roses on fire,
I'll hold you once more, before I tire,
And know your secret,
And ask you for the answer.

White rose
For those few summers only.
A divine acrobat,
A dancer.

B Gilman

SKY AT NIGHT

In the summertime at night
I like to walk under the sky
when it is full of bright stars
and the sky is brilliant moonlight.
I do love that, but I could not explain why,
I feel so happy.
The more I look up to the sky
the more I like it.
It makes me feel that I am part
of this intriguing and so complex planet.
The mystery of the sky at night.
It is so lovely and full of light,
it makes me think how the sky came about.
This firmament is without a doubt
the best display of billions of stars
that give so much lovely light to all mankind.
I cannot help think that God is so great,
without his help the sky would not shine
with all the exquisite light.
Moon, stars and the sun are the most attractive
and wonderful things that are on this earth.
Most of us do not appreciate the lovely things.
God must work hard to make all the beautiful
things in the sky and the earth.
We must praise him for all the lovely things.
The sky at night is my best past time.

Antonio Martorelli

CIRCLE OF LIGHT

When creating the circles,
we guide the journey of our children,
not knowing the moments of life ahead;
providing support to maintain the circle,
hoping as the path of circle grows;
that they will link with other circles;
so creating circles linked by generations,
linked circles are far stronger to
life's moments than squares.

Brian Tallowin

BLACK TULIP

Black Tulip is sad
So her figment falls
Silently opening
Like an umbrella
One by one.

And as daylight
Dawns on her petals
Every pink cloud
Spills a drop of rain,
As high as honey.

In the distance
I hear the calm, beautiful
Delight, of poetic piano chords
One by one.

It is a pitch that moves me.
But Black Tulip is more than sad.

Elizabeth Ryan

TWILIGHT CONE

Miles and miles of them there were
A nightmare with nowhere to turn
Bored brainless sped our helpless pair
Wedged in between the orange glare . . .

Slim sandwiches watched, smug and bored
While teatime treats were packed and stored
As fed up friend marching in and out
To search for guests she was without . . .

When *Roadwork Ends* came into sight
Our stag-eyed pair let out loud cries
Foot firmly down, their speed increased
To lead the pack with relative ease . . .

A crescent moon and twinkling star
Emerged as tired pair parked their car
To gloat as they espied the note
Attached to porch of their approach . . .

Four o'clock is Sunday tea
It stated quite emphatically.
Six miles of cones, x miles an hour,
Resulted in their friendship sour.

Betty Lightfoot

WHEN I GROW UP

I'm going to be a soldier, that's what I'm going to be,
Or how about a sailor and sail across the sea.
I know, I'll be a footballer and win the FA cup,
Or a driver in a racing car, cor, wait till I grow up.

Mum's shouting, 'Are you out of bed? It's time to go to school.'
I think I'll be the headmaster, then I'll make all the rules.
It's really tough being nearly nine, grown-ups have got it made,
'We have to work' is what they say, at least they're getting paid.

If I was paid for going to school, just think what I could buy,
Some football boots, a brand new bike, or a kite that flies so high.
Dad would pay the mortgage, Mum would cook the food,
I could buy them sweeties, it's the least that I could do.

And when I'm all grown up, I'll stay up till half past nine,
Cos, that's what Mummy said I can, when I've a house that's mine.
But wait, who'll do the washing and tuck me up at night?
There'll be *no* Father Christmas, I'll stay a kid, alright!

J Kay

THE SAME TRAP

What kind of friend would I be
If I just sat back and watched
You walk back down that track
You've been there before, oh why
Must you go back for more
For what does she offer you
For you to want to give it all
And live your life on hold for her
How can you sleep at night
Knowing just what she's doing
You know she has another
And she never puts you first
She will never give up what she's got
You will always be a toy to her
But one she's ashamed of
And could never face the world
And that's why it's only now and then
So no-one else can hear
Can't you see she doesn't care
Don't waste your life, not on her

A Houghton

PENNED WITH LOVE

I've worshipped at the temple
Of service and networking
With zeal, both night and day,
From duty never shirking.

I've laboured with my love
For hours on each letter,
Serving the One above
To make life somewhat better.

Always with a gentle touch
Reflecting He who sent me,
The world needs love so much
For aching hearts are plenty.

Compassion is the mantle
I bring to those who're cold,
Their troubles to dismantle
With thoughts both new and old.

If each can bring his candle
To the altar of divinity
All misery we can handle
Of suffering humanity.

Together shedding light
On darkness and obscurity
We shape a future bright
In Spirit's true security.

Emmanuel Petrakis

LOVE OF LIFE

The love of life
Is a graceful bird
Soaring through the evening sky,
The love of life
Is a snow-cap peak
Of a grandiose mountain high.

The love of life
Is a valley serene
With nature's calm,
Where the beasts of the fields may wander,
Knowing nought of harm.

The love of life
Is a child's smile
Innocent and clean,
The love of life
Is mother, the child smile ever seen.

The love of life
Is a searching mind
With freedom yet to roam,
The love of life
Is a quiet time
In the peace of a place called home.

And though we may ever ponder
On the troubles of mankind,
If time and thought for all, we gave,
The love of life we'd find.

L Baynes

WHEN I SLEEP

I see you clearly, when I sleep at night,
But by day . . . you're out of sight.
For at night . . . a vision comes to me,
Your sweet form, is what I see.
A dream . . . I hope will never end,
Comes my broken heart to mend.
Remaining . . . just one step away,
Gone . . . in the cold hard light of day.

Oh to see you . . . just once more,
Have you love me . . . as you did before.
Two souls that merged . . . in harmony,
Two lovers that walked . . . on life's highway.
Sharing, caring . . . bringing pleasure,
Building memories . . . we could treasure.
Those memories, in my heart I keep,
But I see you only . . . when I sleep.

M Muirhead

SHE SLEEPS PEACEFULLY NOW

Rusty pipes, damp walls,
Thin carpet, dead chill.
Tobacco smoke, green mould,
Lying in a sweat pool.
Smashing glass, little stoned thieves,
Dad is out of his head.
Awake at 6am, listening to the screams
The sheets are wet again,
Another black mark, another bruise.
Beat her until she cries
Beat her again harder,
Beat her until she dies.

Paul Willis

COURAGE

       Come to me. I hurt so.
       Pity me. I hurt so.
Still my mind, and do not leave
Me alone, alone to grieve.
Take my heart to gently hold,
While the slame of life grows cold.
Why, as days each one must end,
So must life, my elusive friend?
       Come to me. I hurt so.
       Pity me. I hurt so.

       Come to me. I'm afraid.
       Come to me. I'm afraid
No, don't leave; please turnabout.
Stay! The light is going out.
It's so wretched all alone,
Facing this juncture on my own.
Please don't go. I'm not ready.
Hang on. Please wait. Please don't leave me.
       Come to me. I must go.
       Come to me. I must go.

Donna Fitzsimmons

LAVENDER FIELDS

Fields of lavender - purple and mauve,
Set close in hedgelike rows.
Slim grey stems of stately stature
Ranged in fragrant splendour.

Growing wild in ancient times
In inaccessible places,
The sunny Mediterranean climes
Unveiled this piquant essence.

Happy helpers gather now
In cultivated regions.
Filling their baskets to the brim
With harvest of the season.

Culinary artists tend to achieve
Perfumed sugar and lavender tea,
Crystallised flowers with lavender taste,
Recipients fondly appreciate.

Old-fashioned ladies, in old-fashioned days
Depended on scented spices.
Toilet water, cologne and oils,
Preventive swooning devices.

Charming gifts with lavender made,
Perfumed pillows that will not fade.
Bouquets with aromatic base
Sprinkled in drawers of linen and lace.

Joy M Jordan

WILL YOUR LOVE LIVE?

Will your love live when I'm gone away?
Will it endure when I'm not there to say?
Can love live on although we're far apart?
Will there be comfort for my broken heart
As I live through my pointless day?
   So many times I wish to say;
   How often do I kneel and pray
   In spite of apathy's upstart,
   Will your love live?
When I look up the sky is always grey,
I wonder if you'll ever stray.
And in the theatre of my heart,
Though I may play a leading part
Will you attend my matinee?
Will your love live?

Frank Keetley

THE HIDDEN TOY BOX

The children fell asleep in the wood
After playing
So silently the little teddies
          Come out from the wood
With a compass
And a map of buried treasure
The teddies followed the map
Then they stopped and started
Digging and sweating
Thirsty and hungry, but at last they'd found a toy box of treasure
The children awoke
Happy, dancing teddies and children
Oh what a party they had
Until Mummy said it's time for bed

Jennifer Dunkley

FORCE FIGHT

Come back, stay, please stay
Other world calls out
Take good care of the situation
Force fight night and day

Happy day washed sins away
Come back, please stay
Sew on all those buttons
Ten buttons can fasten all

Need to free-wheel international call
Take it all to heart
Come back, please stay
Force fight hard news day

First in English underneath that
Thought it was Under Milk Wood
Leaving home late at night
Snow falls over the garden

Battery life at the top
Cherry leaves stuck to my feet
Pierced through the heart
First in English underneath that

All that glisters they claim
Life is as it should be
Clear air sparkling champagne
First in English underneath that

Go all the way friend
Leave nothing out all is not lost

S M Thompson

NEW YEAR RESOLUTION 2000

The new millennium, what will it bring?
How to celebrate, how to welcome it in.
Do we sing, will church bells ring?
I know I'll be by the telly at home
Looking to see what's on at the Dome,
Hoping London's panorama is shown
With fireworks - detonations (triggering fright)
Gorgeous illuminations - for visual delight.
I'll see two thousand comes in all right.

Jan Hiller

No Answer

Will you let me say I love you
Will you listen just once more
Can you hear me when I tell you
Will you sigh and close the door.

Are you distant now - as always
Did you ever really care
Shall I listen when my heart says
You were never truly there.

Did you always feel the burden
Did I always love too well
Are you happy in your heaven
Shall I always be in hell?

Margery Fear

Late Autumn

When the last sunny days are ended, and the air
grows keen and cold;
when the last harvest strips the fields of gold,
and apple-boughs are bare;

still the late sway of autumn will not cease
on down and fold;
and as the gathering shadows grow, they hold
unchanging peace.

Fay Marshall

PERPETUITY

The mother, the child, and the child's child,
does the same love rise within each one's breast
and is the birdsong which echoes on and on
the same as heard by listeners in years long past
by the child, the mother, the 'once a child'
who bore the mother?

Is the ephemeral rose as those which flowered
in days beyond recall, adorning other gardens
in lands far distant, borne from its same
primeval seed?

Is it the same sun which shines, has shone,
on our days of good or ill, timelessly setting
to open up the path for the rising moon, whilst
darkness closely harbours growth of the arcane
seed of life?

Eternal One, whose yearning is that all of worth
should mould the one perpetuating truth guide us
to discern this source of love

And if our eyes are blind, grant vision to our minds.

Louise Rogers

THE WEDDING

At last the great day arrives
People buzzing around like
Bees in busy hives

All the planning, thought
And care
To make this day perfect,
For all to share

The bride looks lovely
In her white
Make sure the groom is not in sight

The bridesmaids with their
Silken tresses
Look like film stars in their dresses

The page boy, dressed with loving care
He hopes his mates aren't
There to stare

The bride's mother in her
'Blush' pink looks gorgeous
As she sips her drink

The bride's father in his
Top hat and tails
Looks the best of all
The males

The relatives, so many
That their talking cause a din
But then, at a do like this
You need all your kith and kin

The wedding cars arrive
All polished, shining bright
They put all the other
Cars to shame
While creating quite a sight

The proud father leads
His daughter to the last
Car left in line
Hoping that the driver
Gets them to church on time

The rest have gone before them,
It's been like a busy station
They had to get there earlier
To form the congregation

They march down the aisle
Adjusting their paces
While smiling at the sea of faces

The organ plays 'Here Comes The Bride'
Until they reach
The bridegroom's side

The bridegroom's smile
Is a little bleary
The effects of last night's
Too much beery

The best man looks like
He's in a daze
And sees things only
Through a haze
Looks great in all his
Wedding gear
But no idea what he is doing here

The two of them approach the altar
Determined steps that do not falter
The vicar, resplendent,
In his regalia
Tells them this marriage
Must not be a failure

The ceremony over
They've taken their vows
Now everything that was
His and hers is now ours

They've signed the register
The bells are ringing
They leave the church
With choir singing

The photographer is waiting
To snap the happy pair
While guests are wishing
Them good luck and a
Happy life to share

They brave the storm of confetti
While racing for their car
They are off to the reception
And a welcome drink at the bar

They greet the guests as they arrive
Aunt Sue, and uncle Ted
And here comes cousin Charlotte
And her brother cousin Fred

As they greet the young and old
They hold hands and feel
United by their bands of gold

The cake is cut, the speeches done
There's nothing more to say
So tell the band to play on
And we'll dance the night away

James Valentine Sullivan

READY FOR LOVE?

A little girl stands
Ring-pull in her hand,
Feelings of love forgotten;
Childish love, unblossomed
Happy to be a child.
Is she ready for love?

A teenager stands
Meaningless words in her hand,
Feelings of love unheard of;
Forgotten before remembered
Alone in a lonely world.
Is she ready for love?

A growing girl stands
Temptation in her hand,
Feelings of love unconnected;
Desperate for affection,
Acceptance and emotion.
Is she ready for love?

A young woman stands
Empty dreams in her hand,
Feelings of love unbearable;
Unrequited and unrewarded
Wondering if her time will come.
Is she ready for love?

Sarah Bradley

THE BLOND HORSE LADY

In Drumagarner in the county of Derry, a slim blonde lives since
childhood days
The horses were the only things she loved, her mother wishing her to be
a lady,
Forget the horses, that's what men look after, not nice girls like you but
talk as she may
Collette's love was for horses first, one day when out riding round,
Swatragh, it got foggy, not a nice person could she see to talk to,
done a quick turn to home she did go.
That night to a dance she went and met John Duncan from the
Ballycastle area, she decided he was different from the local lads.
They met several times, she had fallen in love with him, when he said,
'Collette, will you be mine?'
'Aye, surely, what do you think?'
John being calm though awhile.
Being an O'Neill she thought John might go back to the shore.
They got married and are blest with two girls.
John decided they would be educated like their ancestors
not fond of a cob like mother.
He said they are Duncans not like the O'Neills who fought many a
battle in days of yore to rule our country.
When the cob is stopped it will move off.
Collette shouts, 'Woo, woo, you'll not beat me,
I'm an O'Neill even though I'm a Duncan now.'

Mairead McKeever

SHEPHERD'S DELIGHT

Along leafy lanes of summer
With my sweetheart I did go,
Hand in hand we strolled together
With lazy steps and slow.

Mid-winter when we last met
The months slipped slowly by,
I am virtuous and chaste now,
Explaining with a sigh.

We watched the fiery sunset
And kissed like lovers do,
My cool response subdued him
As from me he withdrew.

He took me in his arms again,
His words were warm and tender,
As sun was sinking westward
No sky could match his ardour.

Gazing long upon his sad face
His blue eyes shone with candour,
A lump now came into my throat
He had pierced through my languor.

So suddenly my heart gave way
In the dusky evening light,
Love broke through my shy reserve,
I belonged to him that night.

Betty Mealand

THE CAT PEOPLE

The Cat People are everywhere
Absorbed in my dreams
The essence of restlessness

Eyes reflecting in the half-light
They prance and swirl in patterns
Until a pretty man with wild eyes smiles politely
His voice almost brittle
As he whispers words of reassurance

The Cat People come and go
But they are always there
Waiting quietly as they bleed with emotion
Surrealist pleasure
I am devoured by Cat People

Taylor Parr

THE OLD SCHOOL HALL

The old school hall
Has a pointed roof
And long majestic windows
Letting sunlight through
Shining on a wooden floor
And childlike ghosts
Of children no more

The iron railings
And old stone wall
A majestic domain
Ghostly voices calling my name
Come in they say
Open the door
Its playtime again
Of games no more

Anna Moore

VANISHING YOUTH

I look in the mirror, and what do I see?
A sort of reflection, is that really me?
Two eyes and a nose, a mouth with a grin
And if you look closer a nice double chin
Two ears that are pointed, one south and one north
With wrinkles and crinkles that duly come forth
When gravity takes over you don't stand a chance
The things you were born with no longer enhance
First boobs then your bottom aim straight for the floor
Then the curves and your sex appeal head straight for the door
The moral of this is a sad tale of woe
Give up, breathe out and let it all go.

D Hart

THE LITTLE LASS

The little lass, shiny blonde hair
A picture too see,
Her picture on the wall, proud of her
A smiling baby face has she

She lives on the estate, mother just
Shouts at her
She knows in her mind, that things could
Be better

Mummy, stop and look at my clothes
And look at me
I just want to be loved like anyone
Else you see

Daddy takes me out, he does the best
He can do.
Safe and happy, when the weekend comes through

Ice-creams, feeding the ducks, playing in the park
And a hand guiding her safely
Enjoying the weekend, hoping it goes
Very slowly

I know Daddy loves me, I wish Mummy would
Also love me too
She wipes the tears from her face and sees the
Sun shining through the window

She waves Dad goodbye, hearts
On both sides
To see you again, she dries the tears from
Her eyes

John Raymond Grainger

OVER AND DONE!

It is inevitable - that I must go,
I will leave my love - to all I know,
The strangers too - that I did not meet,
Tell them all - that life's been sweet,
One thing regrettably - that I shall miss,
Is the heart-warming touch - of your sweet kiss,
I must go - I regret that I cannot stay,
The time is now - I won't be far away,
I will look back - on all I have done,
And thank the Lord - for it has been fun,
I won't be alone - so do not grieve,
It will not be the end - when I have to leave,
My life with you all - on this earthly sod,
Will not compare - with the realm of God,
I hope that you will not - think too badly of I,
We will meet again - so for now *goodbye!*

John L Wright

MILLENNIUM MOOD

True to the pattern of progress
Predictably fantasy fraught
Blindly we applaud and passionately
Extremes are relentlessly sought
Privileges and pressures unsustainable
Invariably dearly bought,

Ruled by the frolics of progress
Of change, rearrange and respond
We comply with computered directives
We wave the patriotic wand
Golden handshakes, Mars and Moonstruck
Have peaked but still probe beyond,

Grant one thing changes not in an era
Progress will doubtless win
Never dormant it broods, ever restless
Vibrating with energy within
Disaster, exploit and challenge
Any other would be a grave sin.

Jack Pritchard

THE BARBER SHOP

It's now 3.30 and the kids are out of school
We sharpen up our reflexes and oil all our tools.
In walks Timmy fidget, his pocket full of sweets
It's the only way Mum gets him here with bribery and many treats.
My colleagues are on a go-slow, they know who's next in line
It looks like Timmy Fidget is mine, all mine.
So I sit him in the chair and already he's moving about
He's pulling on the barber's gown and screaming let me out.
His mum gives the instructions for a very complicated cut
Knowing it would be easier to shoe a horse at full gallop.
Anyway I make a start and the battle soon begins
Tears are rolling down his face and the hair sticks to his chin.
Scratch; scratch, scratch, as my scissors swoop and dive
Mum gets him in a headlock, so I can level up the sides.
Timmy's colour goes from red to blue as Mum tightens her grip
Nervously I trim around his ears praying that I don't slip.
And as I reach his fringe Timmy's head drops to his knees
The hair clippings then go up his nose and loudly he starts to sneeze.
After several near misses and a cut that's half complete
Timmy gets hysterical and his face turns white as a sheet.
With a momentary silence it was the final straw
Little Timmy fidget is sick all over the salon floor.
By this time his mum decides that it's time to call it a day
So I clean him up, take the money and send them on their way.
It's the hardest four-pound-eighty that I will ever earn
It's also very amazing that some parents never learn
That if they have a Timmy fidget spare a thought before we start
And please request a normal trim and not a work of art.

Paul Copestake

HISTORY AND I

A moment lapse . . . Enough!
'Neath transient sky of sombre ray,
distorted shadows probe
among cool embers from this dying day.

The half moon weeps . . . as though
enlisted to illumine all;
from scene of twisted steel,
and shattered screen. In mercy night shall fall.

Who will observe . . . and mourn?
Hosts gather unseen to reclaim,
through whom their master now
commands to rise amidst the smoke and flame.

History tends . . . 'tis done!
New owners reap this 'passing by';
bedfellows cloned in time;
unwilling partners, history and I.

A second, two . . . no more;
microbes from waters rushing on;
for what would be, became;
the spectre due, is here, then quickly gone.

Must it be so? . . . Can I
re-live-erase the dreadful scene?
What harm if years I yield,
in lieu of fleeting seconds once have been?

A moment lost . . . to know,
this night oblivion woo'd the slain;
the innocent enshrined
in history . . . and I alone remain.

David Watts

HOLIDAYS

Holidays are the safety valves in our regime of toil;
A time to relax, to come off the boil.
We see them as the signposts of our lives ahead,
Setting a target to aim at whilst we earn our daily bread.
Vacations take all forms and are not always languid and lazy,
Some follow pursuits others regard, when they are resting, as crazy.
Stretched out on the beach we are not all envious of the mountaineer
Who is hyped up with a grimace and a soupçon of fear.
Our main worry being not to overdo the sun and become too pink,
We mainly like to enjoy our break with a smile and a drink.
We all try to 'change the scene' at least once a year
As long as the frequency causes no threat to our career.
The world is now a much smaller place it seems
With rapid transport and better access, it is easier to fulfil our dreams.

Allen Jessop

EARTHWORM

Stretching my fleshy body contracting
it again,
I move through warm, soft, fragrant
earth my body feels its rain.

Scrumptious roots are there full of
food,
water trickles down and I have a shower
underneath a verdant wood.

Heavy thuds clump down above my head,
I hope it's not the machine that I
dread.

Whose blades come down, rotate and
chop me up,
into a dozen pieces waiting for the
birds to sup.

When tiny feet patter about like rain,
some of us come up to the top and find
it's all in vain.

So far I have only been a clone,
when someone's spade cut me in half
now, I am not alone.

Jean Paisley

THE QUIET SCENE

In the loom chair where she sits today
While idly brushing at her hair
Gazing in the mirror she scarcely
Sees the fittings she'd chosen with care

The luxury bedroom was reflected
Full of the colours that she loved
How comfortable she murmured
Still brushing her hair from above

But how boring! Nothing ever
Happens here in this room, she thought
Peering in the mirror she gasps
Aloud at the sight she had caught

For in the mirror she had witnessed
Not the familiar bedroom scene
But another setting, quite strange
The most sinister one ever seen.

Terry Daley

THIS JUNK ERA

Junk post wastes trees
Junk foods harm health
Look all around
More junk abounds

Churches decline
Mammon is God
Greed is the spur
Wrong becomes right
Loyalties fade
Power lust rules
Bully boys thrive

Road traffic slows
Rail traffic's cut
Drug traffic speeds
Arms traffic swells

Teaching unrest
School results poor
Apathy breeds
Truancy spreads

Industries go
Work ethic dies
Skills disappear
Benefit's milked

Morals hit low
Children abused
Marriage a joke
Families fail
Homeless increase
Cheap housing falls
Dome budget soars

Cyril Mountjoy

REASON SONNET

Come let us in the light of reasons walk,
Degrade not this totality in lies,
But in right dignity and truth now talk,
About the wherefore of life and the whys.
Let us not condemn, understanding not,
Because we have not wisdom's goodly grace,
For by the trying knowledge is begot,
And once achieved reveals perfection's trace.
Oh now that this would give me true insight,
To see this whole and to declare the same.
Then would that light be fulminating bright
To illuminate and announce your fame.
Thus by excellence of thought and manner,
Would this height become our dearest banner.

Barry Bradshaw

THE FORGOTTEN WAR DEAD

Where were you when we were dying
Anguish and pain rents the air
Arms outstretched we were crying
Help us
Give us hope and care.

Where were you, now we are weeping
Bodies long cold in the ground
Where is our triumphant and glory
All we can see is a mound

Where are you in our darkness
The long ink black of the night
Where is our candle of brightness
Leading us back to the light

P Cauvain

Rock Bottom

Down and out in London,
Living on the street,
Weighing all the pros and cons
Of everyone I meet.

No home, no job, no money,
I've bucked the normal trend;
Cold, and tired, and hopeless,
And fearful of the end.

How did all this happen?
It's difficult to say;
I think it happened slowly;
A little dip each day.

And now I'm past redemption
By any human hand;
For I have touched rock bottom;
I've joined the alien band.

I hope my god will help me;
I know I've lost the plot.
He is my one salvation;
The only one I've got.

V B D'Wit

FEELINGS

I've got this funny feeling,
I don't know what it means,
I think I've felt it before,
Once when I was in my teens!

It makes my heart beat quickly,
It makes me feel confused,
I think I really like it,
But my friends are not amused!

I really do feel happy,
The way I've never felt before,
I rarely see my friends now,
I think they know the score!

The reason for these feelings,
By now you ought to know,
It's love that makes me feel this way,
And now I'm all aglow!

Christine Jane Bennett

IT'S SO EASY TO FORGET

It's so easy to forget, so I remember
From December to December,
I remember your beauty, I remember it's rare
I write in your book, for your garden I care.

I work at remembering, it's easy to forget
I must remember I am always in your debt.
The debt of life which you gave me at birth
The debt of your death for which I found no mirth.

It's easy to forget, so I will remember
In constancy from December to December.
You paid the price we all have to pay
This one big forfeit doesn't move out the way.

Denise Shaw

FOREVER DEAR

Someone who touched my life
Only a while
Who was sweet and intelligent
Warmness and smiles
Who I felt when we met
A closeness and caring
And the few short years
All of the days we were sharing
I learned from you
Thought you were one of a kind
Your serenity touched
My world ever divine
You were special and sadly
You're no longer here
But the memories I have of you
Forever dear
You're someone who had
Touched my life sincere and true
Our world's not the same
Since we have lost you

Jeanette Gaffney

A FAVOURITE PLACE

Cornfields winding down to the sea,
The oak and the cedar tree,
Farm house and Friesian cow,
Seagulls following the plough.
There is no place I would rather be,
Than this Essex countryside by the sea.

The tide's in now, the tide is high,
Boats and swans go sailing by.
Waves are lapping over the green,
The boy has arrived who sells
The ice-cream.

As I walk down the narrow street,
Trodden for generations of weary feet,
The Tudor buildings on the hill,
Standing as if time had stood still,
And as I go down to the quay
It's as if Mathew Hopkins I may see.

This is a favourite place for me
Mistly and Manningtree by the sea.

Vivian Chrispin

SONG OF A SPARROW

What songs of love do the birds sing
To replace the winter gloom with spring
Sit my love and listen well
They sing of times to come
When all will be a land of green
Beneath the warming sun

The chirruping, tweet-tweeting
The treetops where they're meeting
Listen to them all now
Bringing in the day
A world that's ripe to taste good life
Is what they seem to say

Only now in this golden hour
As I pick for her this flower
Can I appreciate more fully
The joy in simple things
The smiling face of the girl I love
And the song a sparrow sings

Rodger Moir

THE SUN

This morning we had frost
The garden's looking sad
My heart has missed a beat
Plants have dropped their heads

The birds have had their seeds
My cat's had to be fed
There's always lots to do
It's time to go inside

Now for work, the sun is out
The plants have raised their heads
Our sun has brought them back to life
Nature, is a wonderful thing

The sun
A daystar
This eye of heaven
Is the elixir of life.

Carole A Cleverdon

WE MUST ACT NOW

Winter, spring, summer and fall
Every year we know the score
But things are changing
For the worst
The ozone's going from our earth
Cancer, drought, starvation too
We say that we care
But this can't be true
Poisons in the sky
Poisons in the seas
Put there by you
Put there by me
Animals dying one by one
If we don't act now
Soon they'll be gone
So take to your heart
All that I say
We must act now, today

Greeny 2000

UNTITLED

Nicholas my loving son,
He makes my life worthwhile,
Even though I'm often sad,
He always makes me smile.
How dull my life would be
Without his PMA (Positive Mental Attitude)!
And his funny little notes that say,
C'mon Mum, brighten the day.

Cynthia McGregor

THE BEAUCHAMP

(In memory of my great grandfather John William Smith and all the members of the crew who lost their lives in the Beauchamp Lifeboat disaster in November 1901)

On a bleak cold night in November, 1901
A north north-east gale was blowing
And the rain was pouring down.
The North Sea was black and heavy
When a flare came from Barber Sands,
The Cockle Lightship fired distress signals.
The hour was just eleven pm, when
The lifeboat crew of *The Beauchamp*
Were all quickly summoned to the shed.
They tried hard to launch *The Beauchamp*
But she was washed off the skids instead.
Straight away another launch was attempted
But warp and tackle had to come to her aid.
About two o'clock in the morning came
Before another launch was successfully made.
The gale was howling with a fearful force,
The rain was heavy, cold and fast,
The Beauchamp was seen to be alright now
So the launchers went home at last.
Only one man remained at the scene
Alone on Caister's desolate shore.
His name was James Haylett Senior - 78 years old.
The Beauchamp was floated and sail made
Towards the signals which were dead to windward.
Battling against the cruel sea, the brave *Beauchamp*
Was plunged back into the black, heaving wash.
She struggled desperately to keep afloat now,
With the crew fighting against the vile storm.
They tried furiously to keep her upright, so
They lowered the mizen and put up the helm.
The Beauchamp tirelessly fought the raging fury.

She was battered and tossed and turned,
Suddenly struck on the starboard quarter
The crew toiled with courage and bravery all round.
They wrestled against the perilous elements
Which tormented them on that bleak night,
But alas, the brave *Beauchamp* was beaten,
She was forced back ending keel up near the shore.
The tenacious crew were tragically trapped now
Beneath the boat in the swirling seas.
The result was the death of those loved ones
The tragic loss of nine brave, precious lives.
All I have left of my Great Grandfather Smith
Is a mourning brooch with a lock of his hair
And the memory he was part of the crew
Who fought so courageously without any fear.
The village of Caister will always remember
With a pride beyond all doubt,
How the crew of *The Beauchamp lifeboat*
In November, 1901, *never turned back.*

Margaret Luckett-Curtis

My Small Country Garden

My small country garden
Some people may consider it just OK
But to me it is paradise, from morning to night,
From springtime to winter,
Tuned close to nature gives me a thrill.
Each flower, bird or tree, he least little thing
Fills me up with delight.
Sure the best things in life
Indeed are all free.
There's the red-breasted robin, bobbing up here and there,
The gardener's friend constantly near.
Many trees offer shelter, from spring showers and hail,
All the flowers wave their petals
In a colourful pastel array.
At night, scented stock perfume the air
With fruit trees of all kinds promising to.
In the cool, early morning, cobwebs hang loose decorating freely
Whatever the spider may choose.
Small dewdrops light up
A ray drawn in such colours,
Ruby red, emerald green, diamonds to all crystal clear.
At the end of the day,
There's the bat and the owl
And I'm not leaving out the tiny field mouse.
In this habitation every creature and plant is ever so grand,
From daylight to night all put on such a show
That I cannot ignore,
Such beauty predisposes my eyes to behold.

Margaret Hurley

CHANCE

Take a chance to love,
Take a chance to smile,
Take a chance to be silent,
Take a chance to forgive,
Take a chance to care,
Take a chance to speak to someone,
Take a chance to help someone in trouble.
Life is a challenge.
Take a chance on it.

J Campbell Jones

I AM WITH YOU

I am with you as you walk in your garden,
Breathing the rose's perfect bloom.
Mists of sweet remembrance swirl soft around us
In autumn's twilight gloom.

Find me in the dew-kissed flowers of morning,
Hold me pressed deep within your heart.
Worry not that death divides us,
In spirit we are always together, not far apart.

We grew older and our needs were changing,
We never knew then, quite what we had.
Never said 'I love you' when we should have.
Now you walk alone and feel so sad.

But in peaceful moments of pensive stillness,
When tempted to fret or maybe even brood,
There comes a whisper gently stealing,
'Only remember when love was good.'

Maggie Nelson

On Going Blind

Let me touch the light and hold the sunshine in my hand
Let me feel the colour of the rose
Let my soul trace the contours of your face
Let my feet leave footprints in the sand.

Give back my heart for just a while and set me free to roam
I'll watch the rainbow paint a halo 'round the Earth
I'll sit among the flowers and cry just for myself
Until I greet the darkness as my home

E V Fox

SUBMISSIONS INVITED
SOMETHING FOR EVERYONE

POETRY NOW 2001 - Any subject,
any style, any time.

WOMENSWORDS 2001 - Strictly women,
have your say the female way!

STRONGWORDS 2001 - Warning!
Age restriction, must be between 16-24,
opinionated and have strong views.
(Not for the faint-hearted)

All poems no longer than 30 lines.
Always welcome! No fee!
Cash Prizes to be won!

Mark your envelope (eg *Poetry Now*) *2001*
Send to:
Forward Press Ltd
Remus House, Coltsfoot Drive,
Woodston,
Peterborough, PE2 9JX

**OVER £10,000 POETRY PRIZES
TO BE WON!**

Judging will take place in October 2001